DISAPPOINTED
MONSTERS

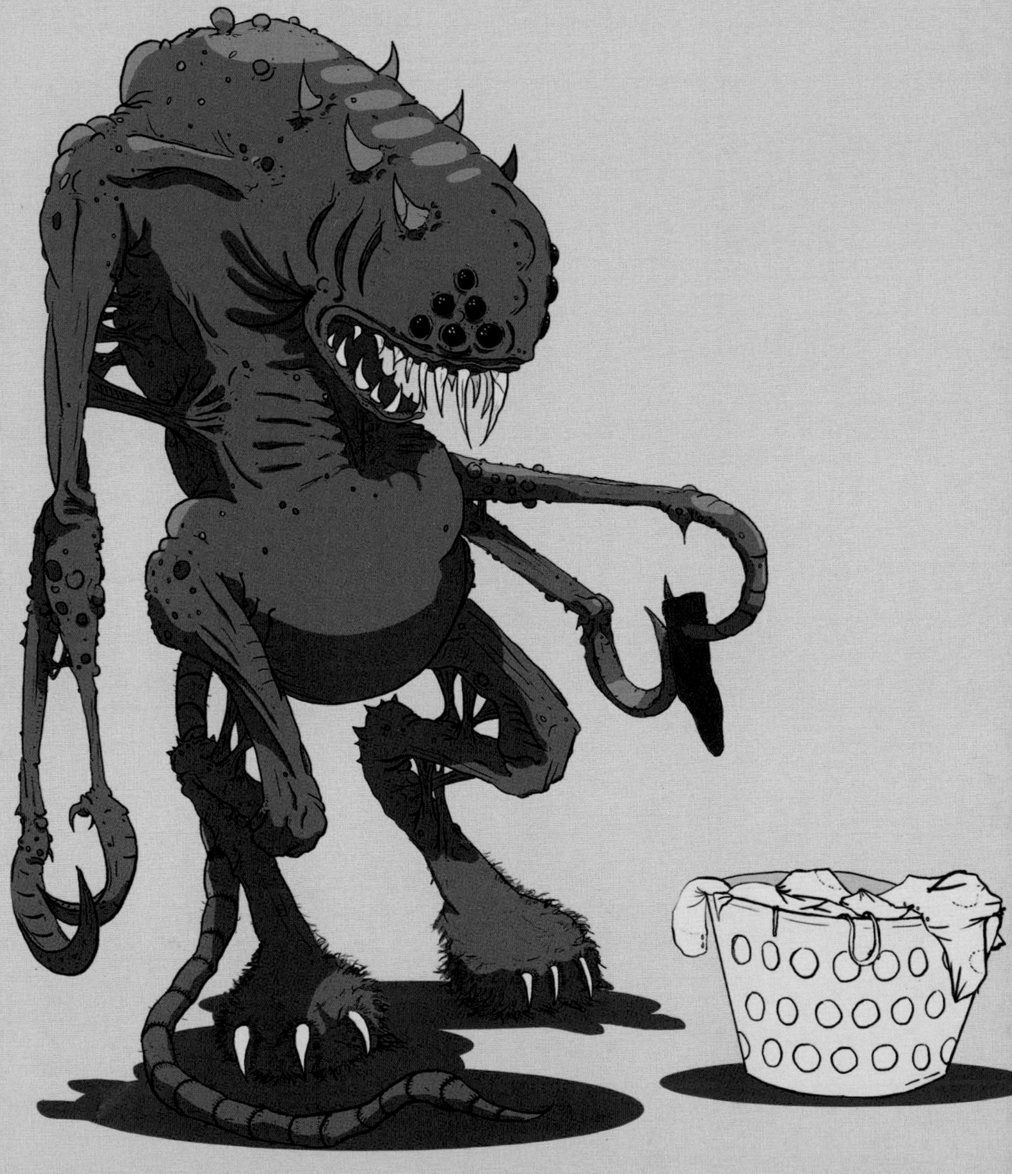

DISAPPOINTED MONSTERS

An A to Z of life's little disappointments

ELI BOWES

AMMONITE
PRESS

With very special thanks to all my friends and
family who supported me while I wrote and
illustrated this book. Many of you have made it
onto the pages inside, but there is no way on earth
I'm telling you which ones ...

First published 2017 by
Ammonite Press
an imprint of Guild of Master Craftsman Publications Ltd
Castle Place, 166 High Street, Lewes, East Sussex, BN7 1XU,
United Kingdom

Text and illustration © Eli Bowes, 2017
Copyright in the Work © GMC Publications Ltd, 2017

ISBN 978 1 78145 323 0

A catalogue record for this book is available from the
British Library.

Publisher: Jason Hook
Design: Robin Shields
Editor: Jamie Pumfrey

Colour reproduction by GMC Reprographics

Printed and bound in Turkey

INTRODUCTION

Whoever we are, whatever we do, there is one
thing we all have in common: disappointment. It is
what turns us all into monsters, but it is also what
makes us human. You will no doubt recognize many
of the everyday setbacks and frustrations this book
contains. By way of making peace with your own
disappointed monsters, we recommend using the
checklists at the back of the book to tick off those
you encounter and to make a list of the many
others who cross your path.

You should also always REMEMBER ...

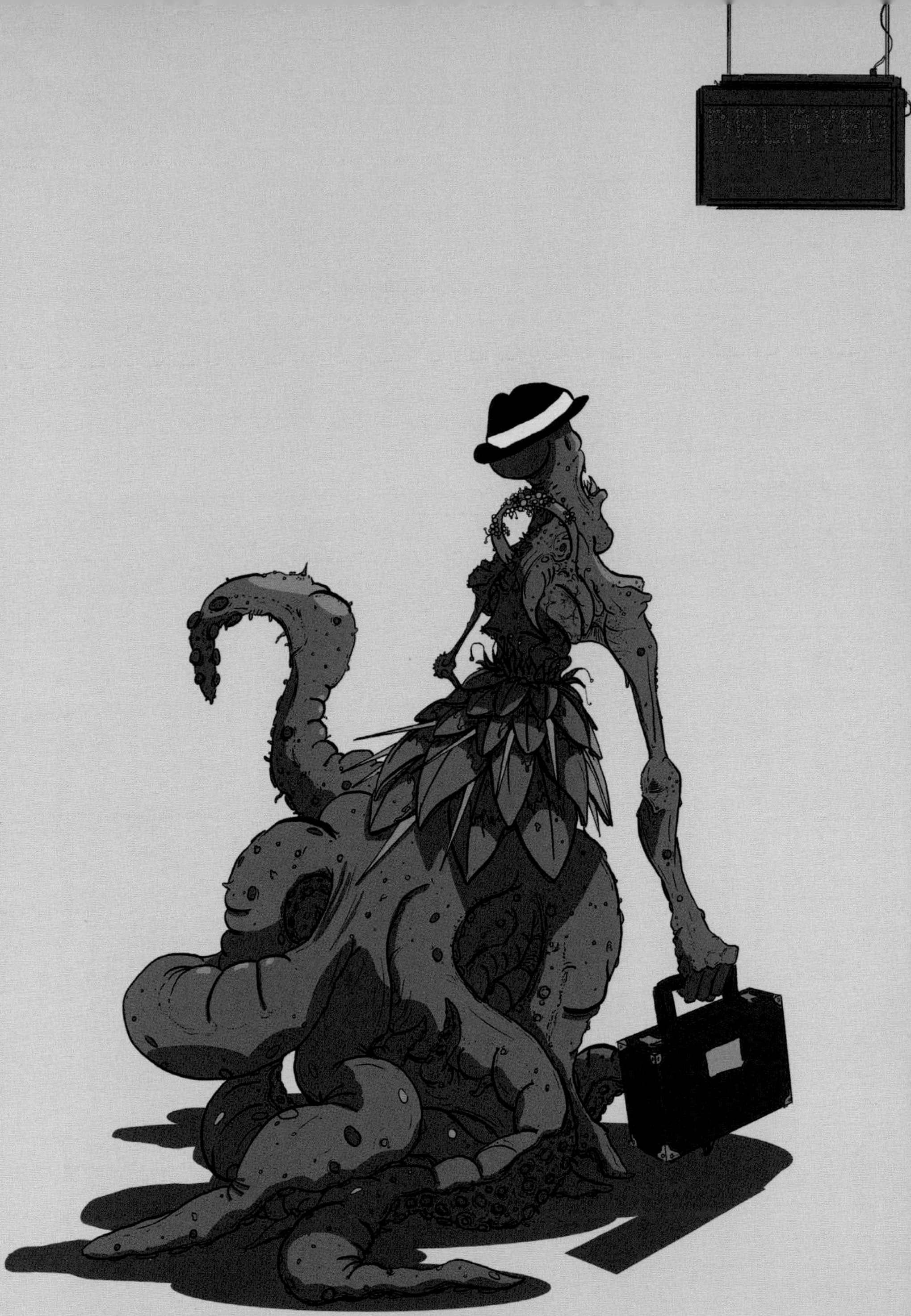
DELAYED

... SOMEWHERE SOMEONE (OR SOMETHING!) SHARES YOUR PAIN ...

is for Alarm

This monster is disappointed.

It forgot to turn the alarm clock off on Friday. Suddenly it is 6:15 on Saturday morning, the radio is on, the clock is flashing and simulated birdsong is tweeting. This is not relaxing. The bin collection truck will be along shortly anyway, so there is no way it will be able to get back to sleep now.

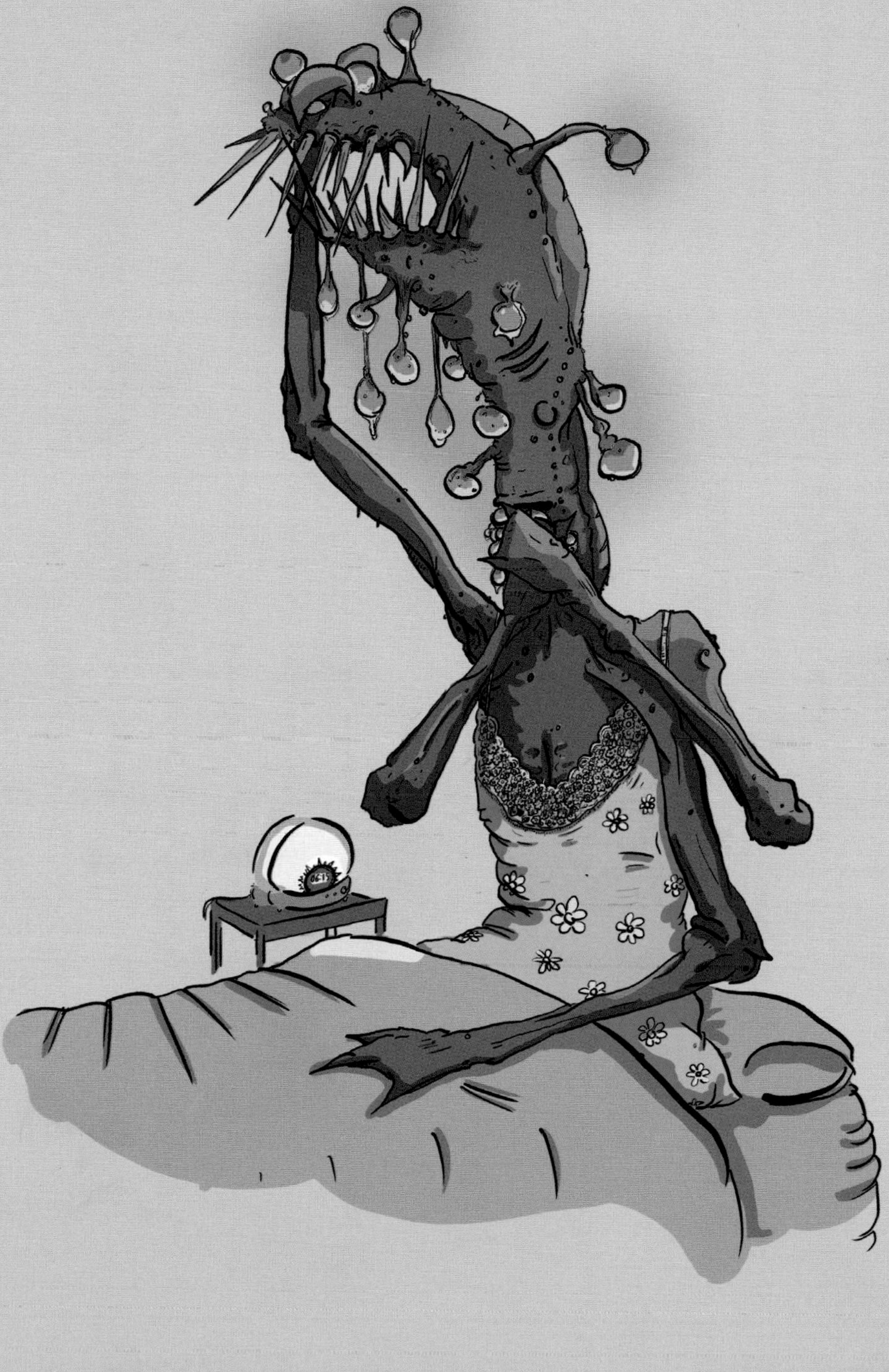
06:15

is for Boiler

This monster is disappointed.

It was having a shower and the boiler
has switched off mid-lather. Now it is
torn between carrying on in icy water or
getting out and re-firing the pilot light.
Either way, the relaxing, calming effect
of its Cherry Blossom and Jasmine Pure
Silk Indulgent Crème de Douche has
been negated.

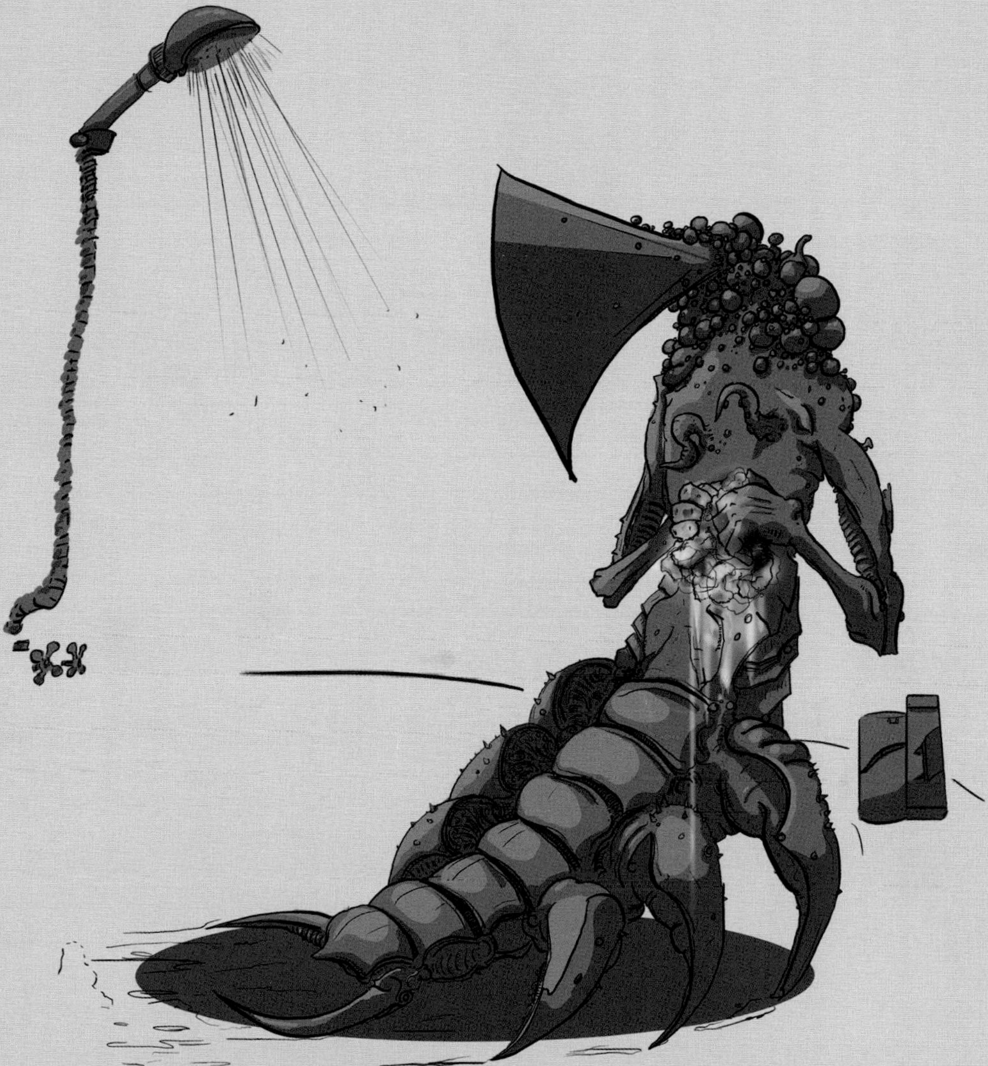

is for Cola

This monster is disappointed.

The fizzy drink it was looking forward
to has gone flat. The lid was screwed
on really tightly and it had only been in
the fridge since last night. There is still
half the bottle left, but there is no point
keeping it now.

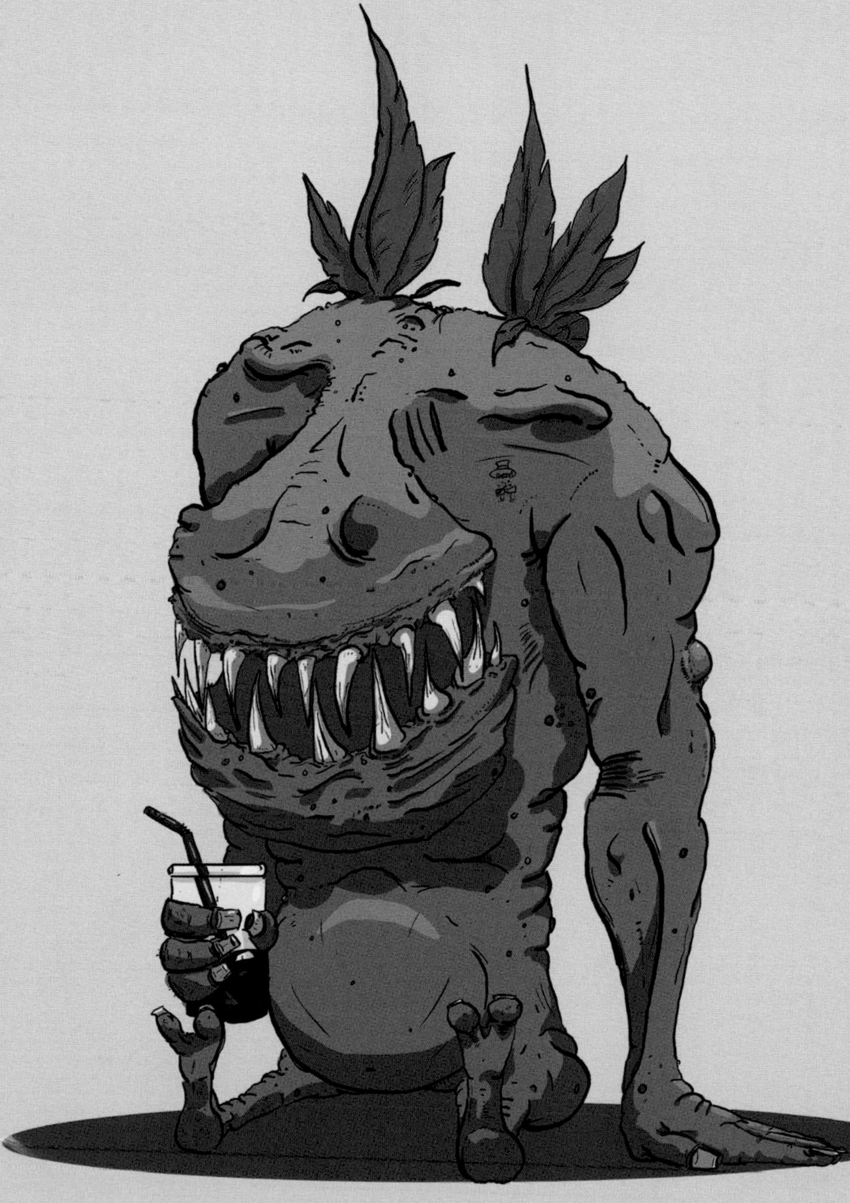

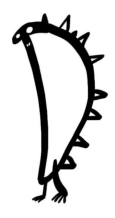

is for Damp

This monster is disappointed.

It has painted the whole bathroom with
expensive damp-proof paint. Again. Yet
still the damp patch in the corner keeps
coming through and making the room
uninviting. It can't relax in the bath
seeing that there.

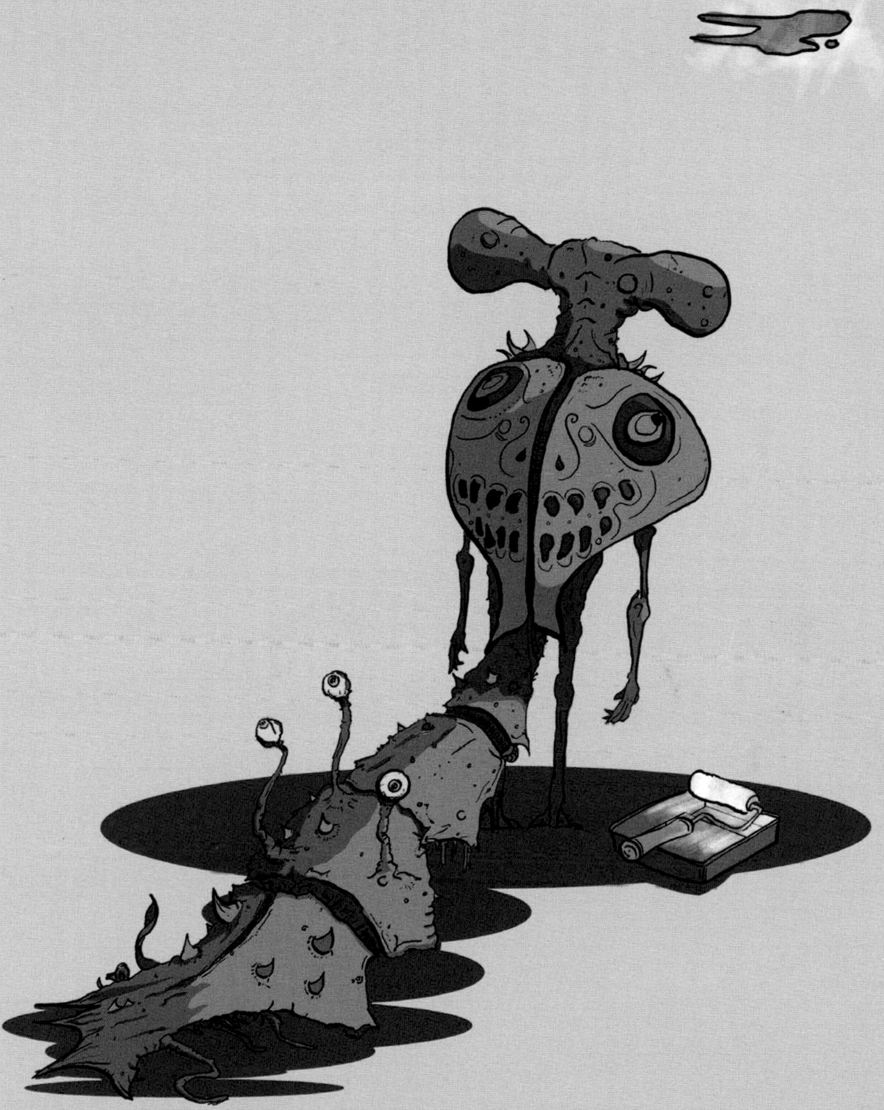

is for Extraneous

This monster is disappointed.

It has spent an entire afternoon
assembling flat-pack furniture. Now it
is late. And there are some worryingly
important-looking pieces left over.

is for Freezer

This monster is disappointed.

It has to defrost the freezer, the ice
build-up has become a problem. It
knows that before it can thaw it with
a hairdryer, it is going to have to eat
frozen peas with every single meal for
the next two weeks. It doesn't even really
like them but it feels wasteful to throw
them away. The bag is still nearly full.

is for Garbage

This monster is disappointed.

The garbage bag it was carrying out
has split. Now there is bin juice all over
the floor. It might be the haddock from
Monday. Now it has to somehow put the
bag in another sack before it can take it
out. Then it will have to mop the floor
and bleach the bin. The haddock was not
worth this disappointment.

is for Handle

This monster is disappointed.

It was making coffee for guests and one of the cups broke. It's a shame as it was expensive South American fair-trade organic coffee and there is none left in the cupboard. Also, the carpet is pale. And the house is rented.

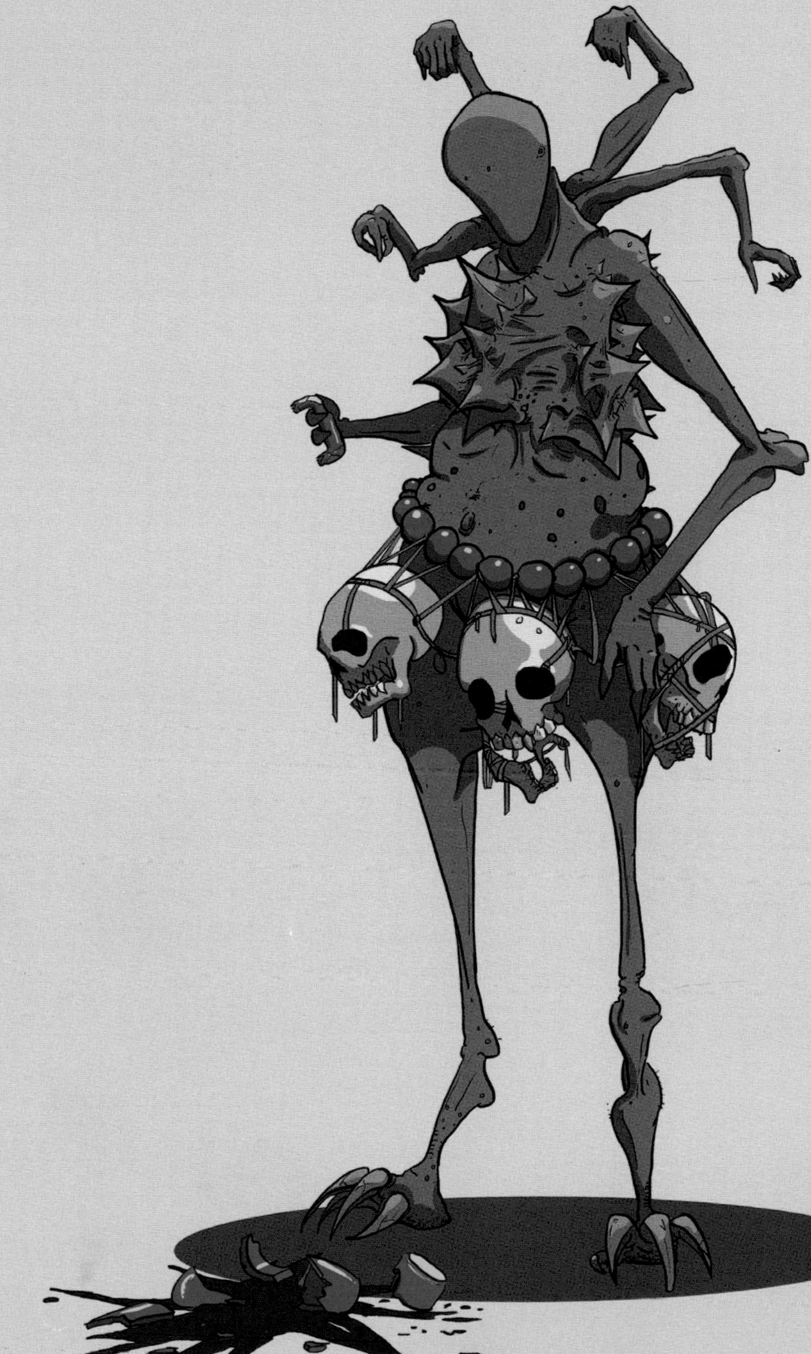

is for Immersive

This monster is disappointed.

It bought two tickets to what was
described as an enthralling, immersive
and seminal piece of interactive,
promenade art / soundscape / theatre
experience. Sadly, it was expensive
and overrated. In retrospect, it was
a terrible location for a first date.

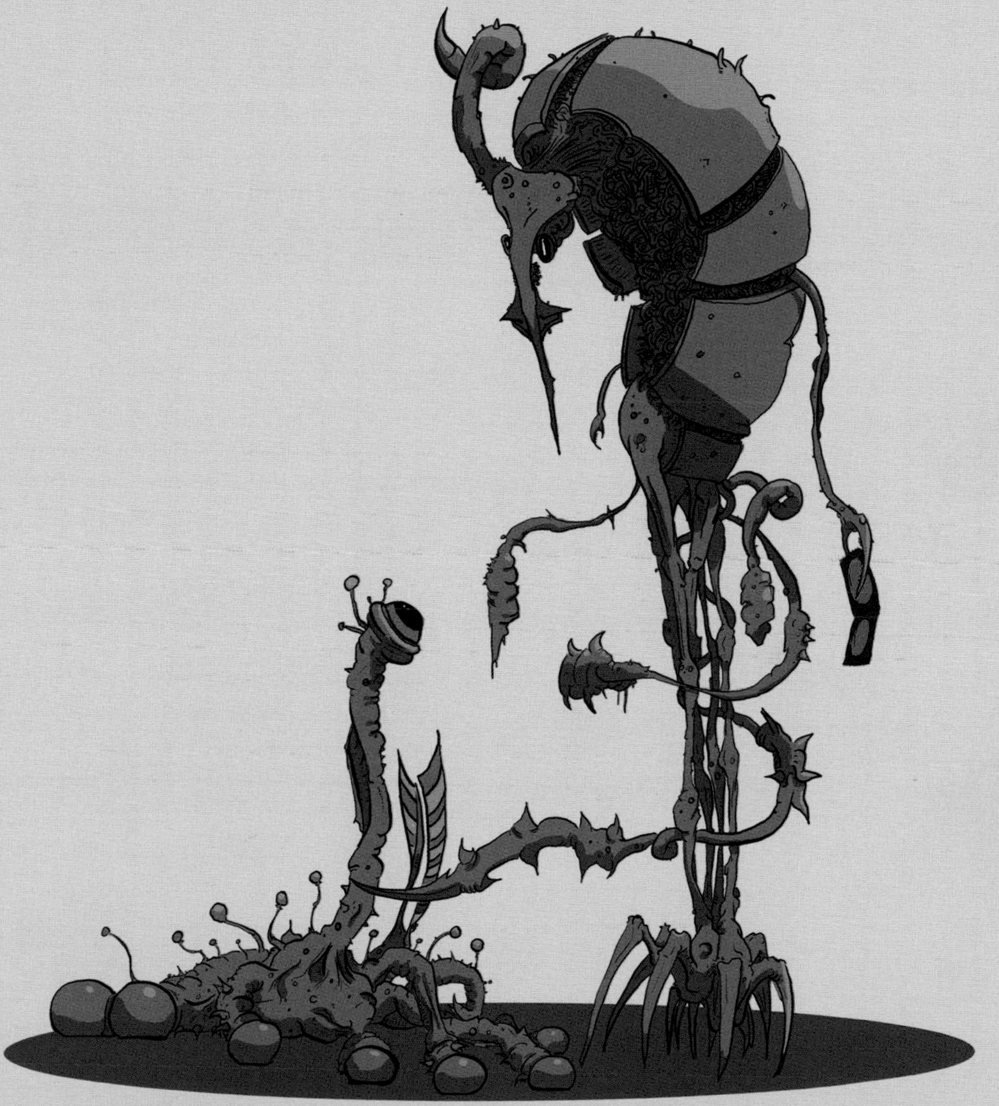

is for Jar

This monster is disappointed.

It wanted to make some toast with
marmalade but whoever last used it
managed to get crumbs, butter and
something that looks like pesto in the jar.
This is disgusting and completely ruins
this monster's breakfast. It has already
toasted the wholesome multigrain low-GI
bread, and for what?

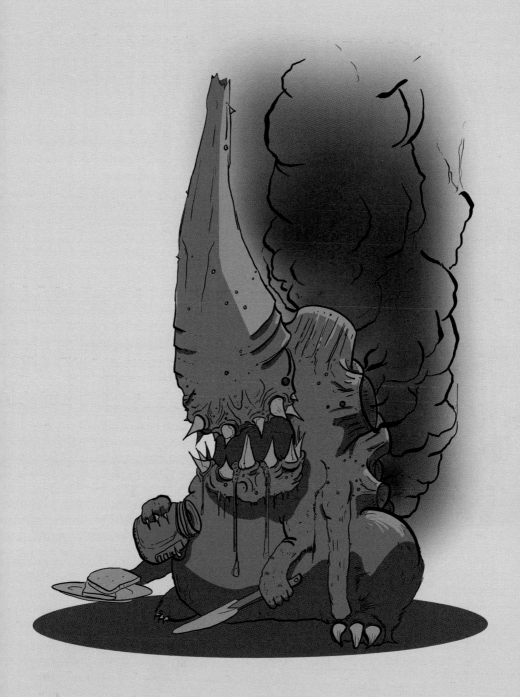

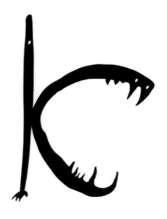

is for Keys

This monster is disappointed.

It somehow let the door slam behind it
and now it is unable to get back in.
It knows it can't reach the handle
through the mailbox, but is trying to
anyway. It really can't afford the
call-out fee the locksmith will charge.

is for Lavatory

This monster is disappointed.

The toilet paper has run out. It thought
that there was a spare roll in the
cupboard under the sink, but there is
not. The spare rolls are in the hallway
cupboard downstairs. Mostly it is upset
with itself for not noticing before it
was too late.

is for Milk

This monster is disappointed.

It was really looking forward to a cup
of tea but the milk has turned. There
is a spare pint in the freezer but that is
of no help to it now. Plus it has already
poured the water onto the teabag, so it is
vexed by the wastage.

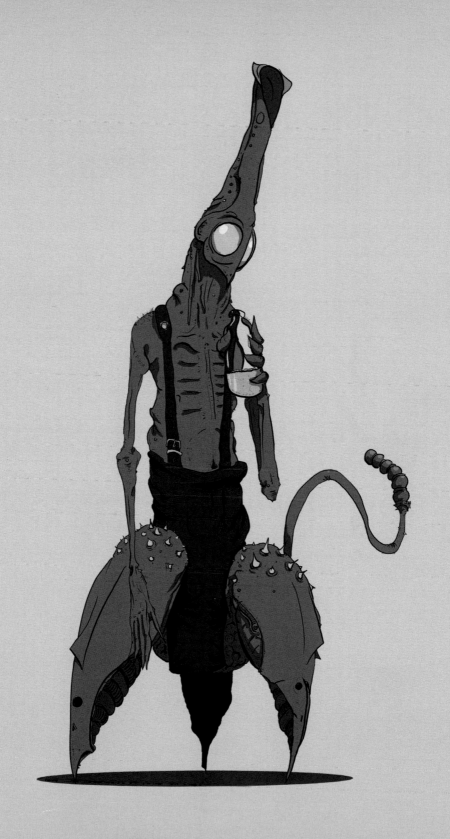

is for Nobody

This monster is disappointed.

None of its friends have come to its
birthday party. They all said they would,
but then no-one came. It bought lots of
pizza, party hats and everything. Now it
is all going to go to waste.

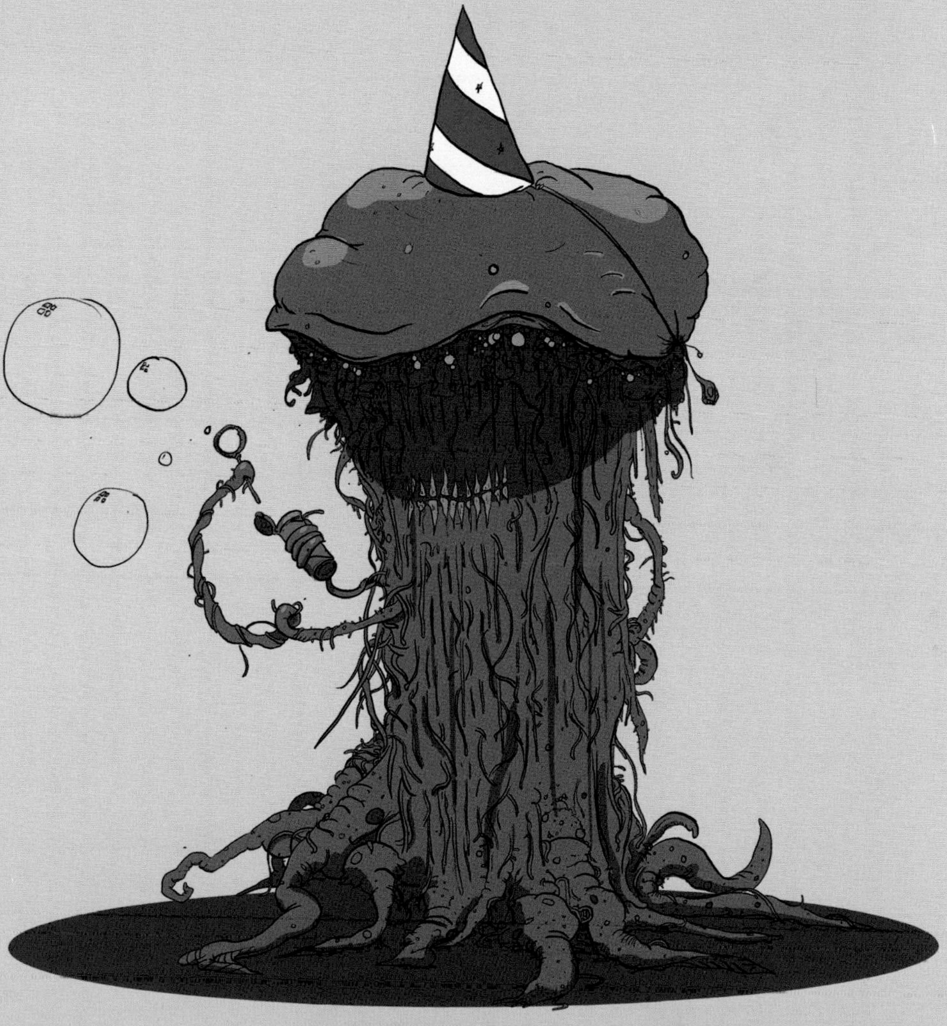

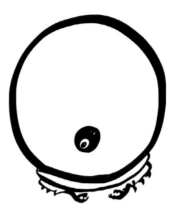

is for Overpriced

This monster is disappointed.

It was hungry and bought a pasty,
while waiting for a train. It was really
expensive and the pasty is very greasy.
It is a bit cold, too, and the filling is
soggy. A most unsatisfactory dinner
that is already resulting in heartburn.

is for Plughole

This monster is disappointed.

It has to remove the disgusting, matted
ball of hair from the plughole in the
bath. It is pretty sure that its housemate
is to blame. It smells really bad, which
is a surprise because the shower gel is
lavender scented.

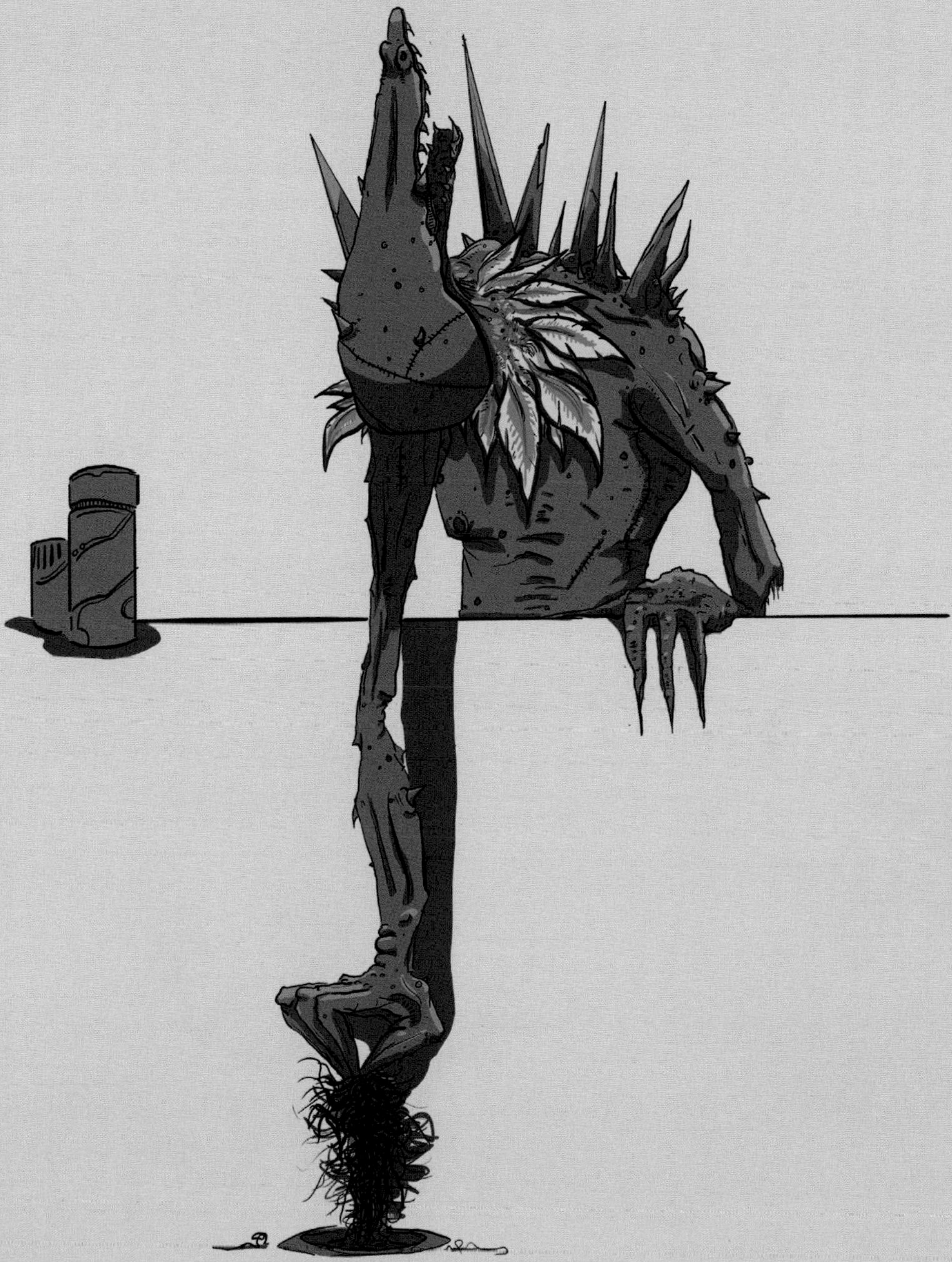

is for Quiz

This monster is disappointed.

The pub quiz team it has joined
has chosen a name that is overused,
clichéd and unimaginative. They
went for 'Quizzard of Oz'. At least
it wasn't 'Quizteam Aguilera'. That
one is really rubbish.

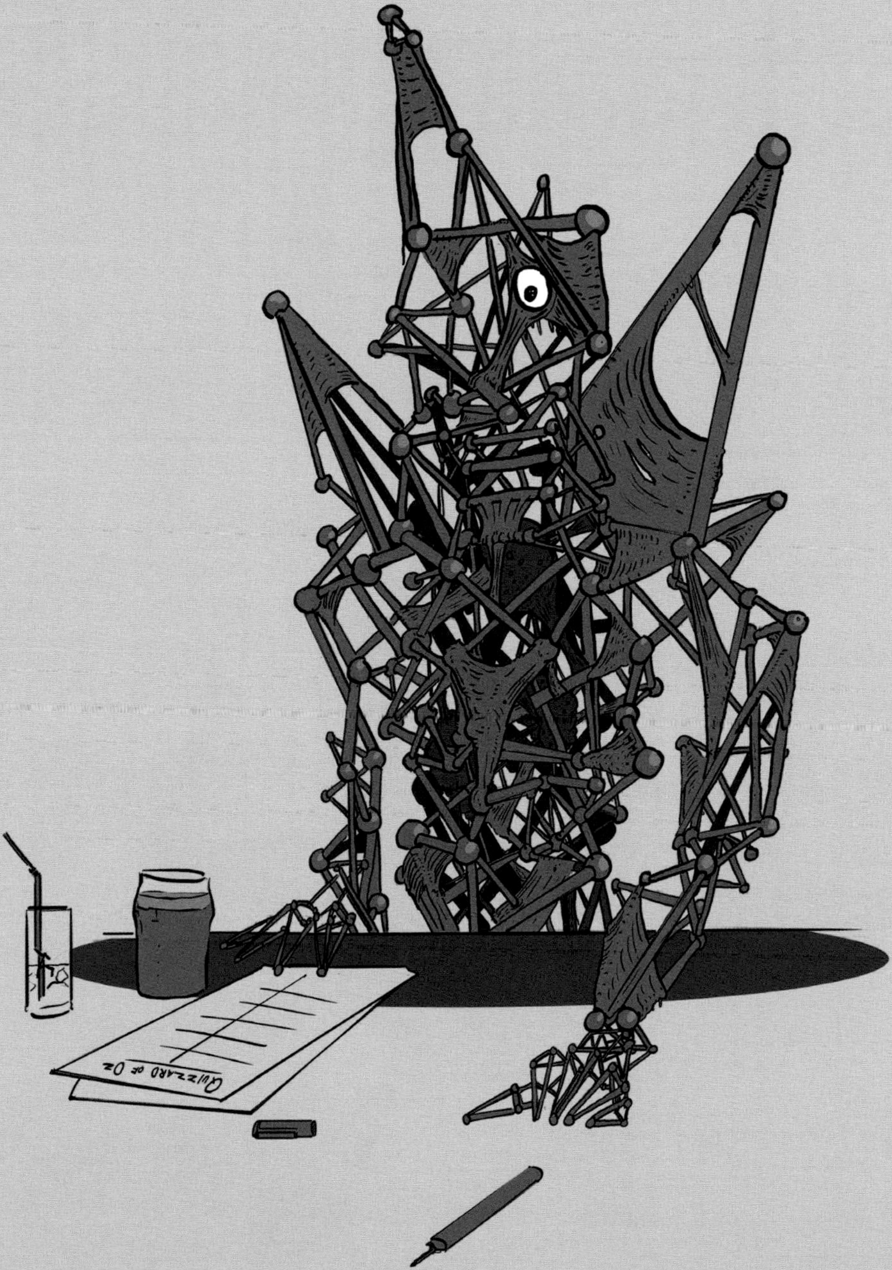
QUIZZARD of OZ

is for Receipt

This monster is disappointed.

It lost one glove and had to buy a
replacement pair. Then, when it got
home, it found the missing glove. It
regrets not having kept the receipt.

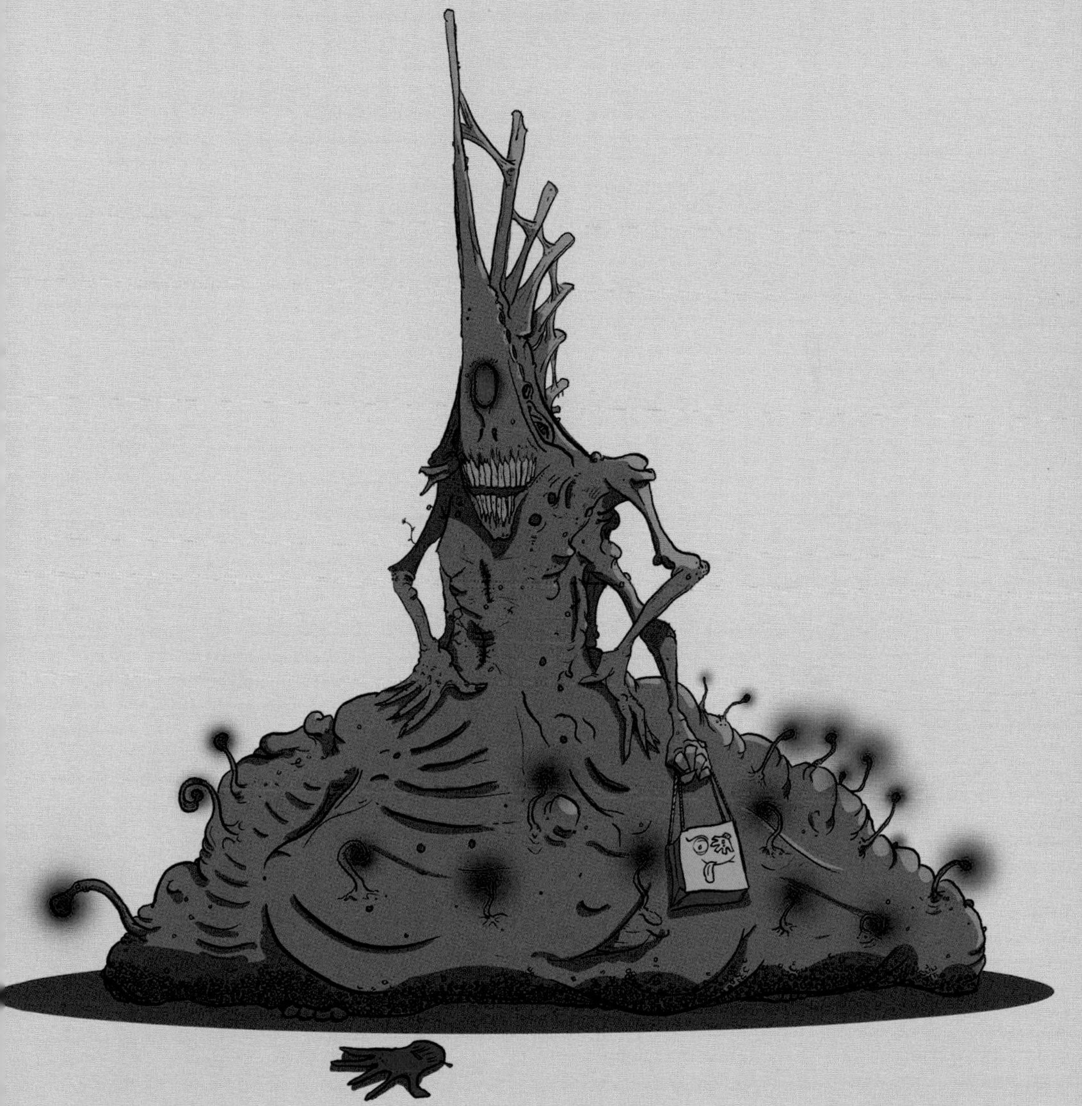

is for Sandwich

This monster is disappointed.

It was eating some lunch before going out to meet friends, and has managed to spill sandwich filling on its favourite vest. Now it will have to change, it might be late, and it has the time-consuming task of handwashing the item when it gets home later.

is for Towel

This monster is disappointed.

It is also wet.

It has just had a shower but has left the towel on the radiator in the hall. Now it is going to have to make do with just a flannel or risk running through the house naked.

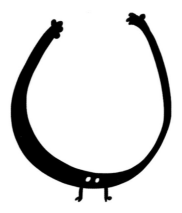

is for Umbrella

This monster is disappointed.

Its umbrella has blown inside out and broken. Now it will get water in its holes and take ages to dry out. The umbrella was an expensive one, too, so the disappointment is twofold.

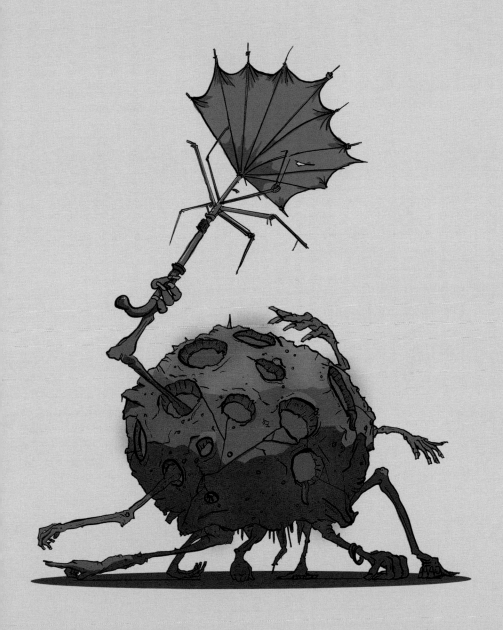

is for Vegetables

This monster is disappointed.

It only just bought this bag of salad,
but it has already gone off. It has
become slimy and is sitting in a smelly,
black soup. It knew this would happen.
This is always what happens when it
tries to eat healthily.

is for Weight

This monster is disappointed.

It has been trying to lose weight,
eating carefully and taking more
exercise, but it has barely managed to
shift any weight and summer is coming.
Now it doesn't want to go outside in
case people stare at it.

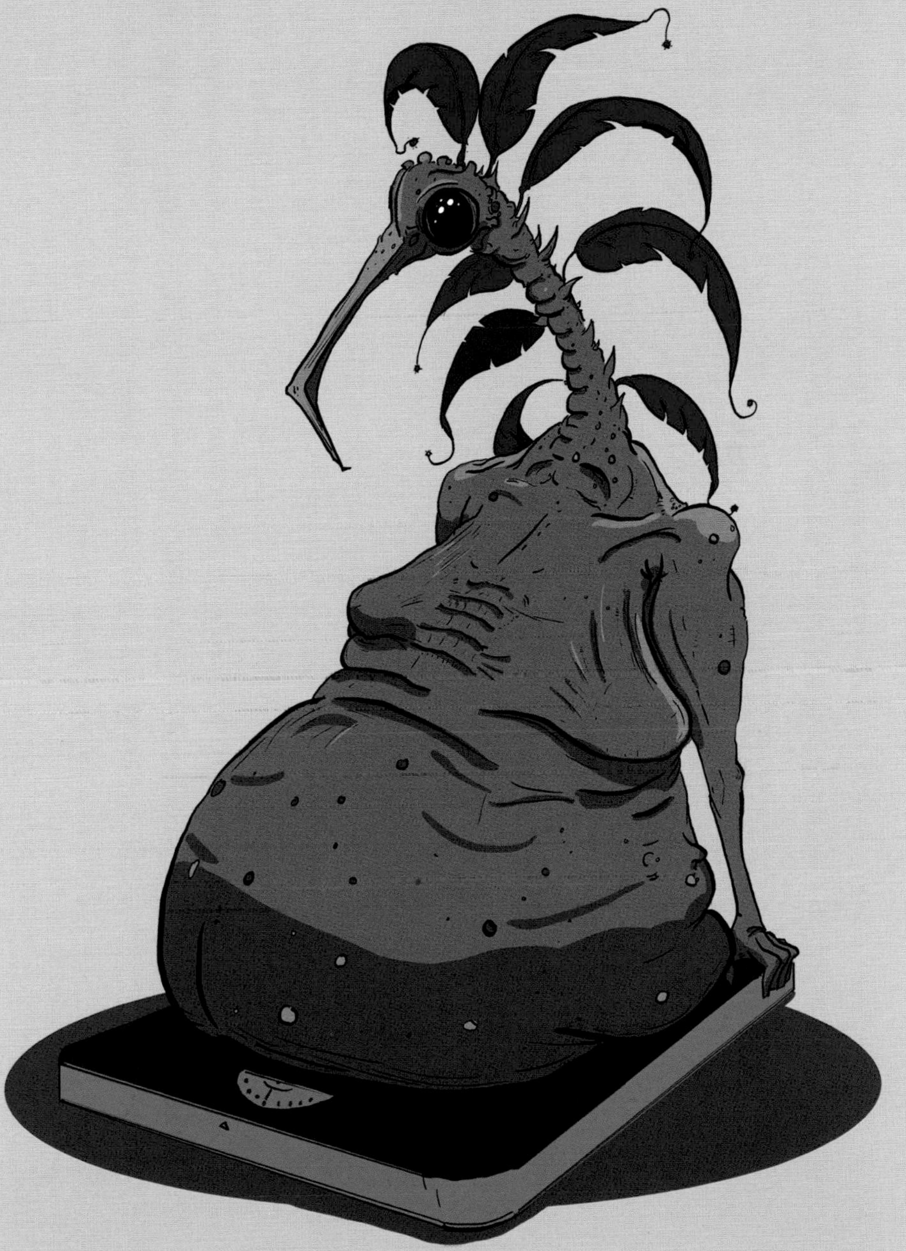

is for Xmas

This monster is disappointed.

It has just switched on the tree lights but nothing happened, now it is going to have to test every bulb. One by one. If only it had tested them before wrapping them around the tree. This never would have happened when it was younger. The tree always looked much more magical then.

is for Yolk

This monster is disappointed.

It has left the last egg in the pan
too long and now it is hard boiled.
It really wanted a soft-boiled egg
and had cut the toast into little
strips specially. Breakfast has
fallen short of the expectations
this monster had placed on it.

is for Zipper

This monster is disappointed.

The zipper on its favourite hoodie
has become misaligned and jammed.
Although it can be fixed, this monster
expected better quality from this
premium-priced American brand.

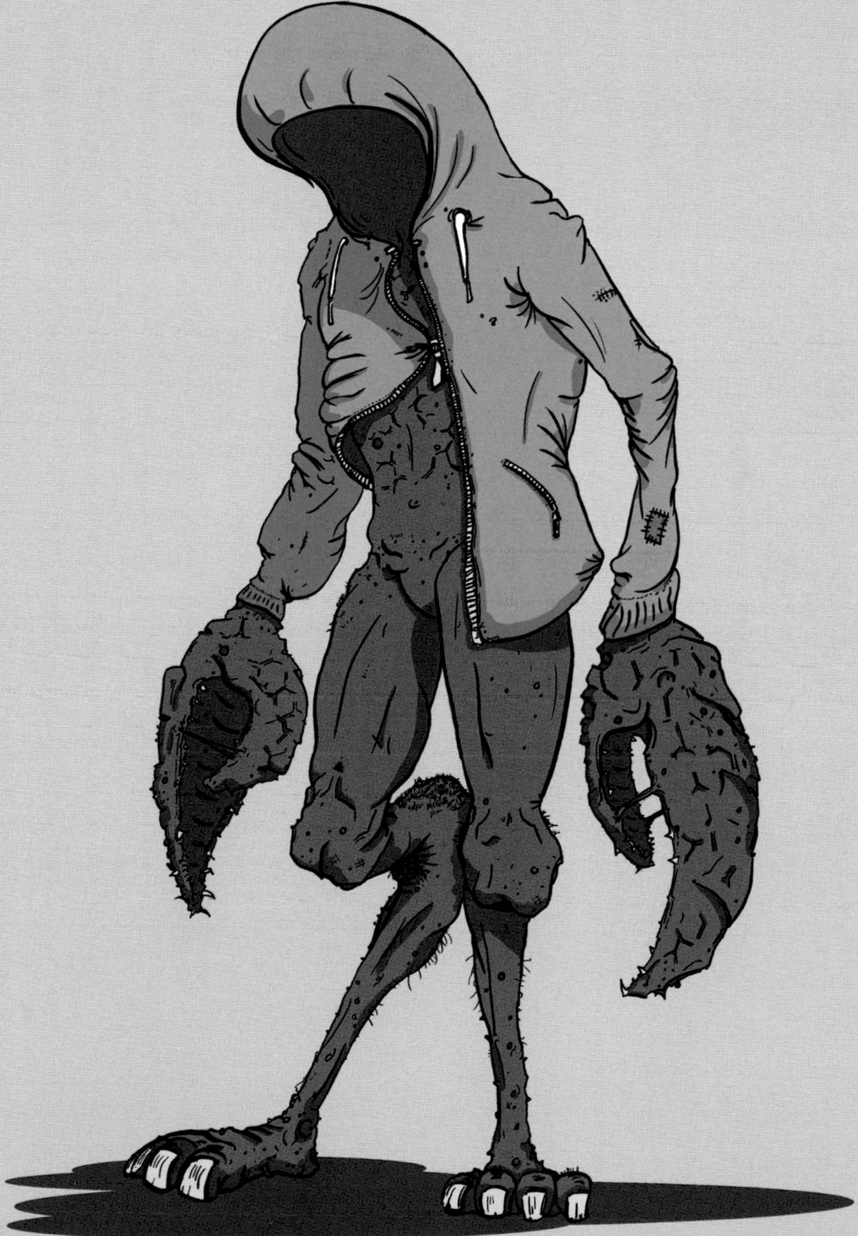

DISAPPOINTED MONSTER CHECKLIST

Tick off your own encounters.

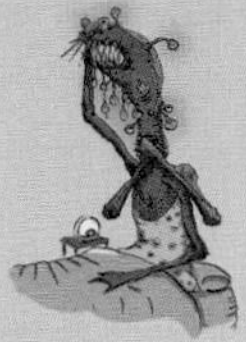

Alarm

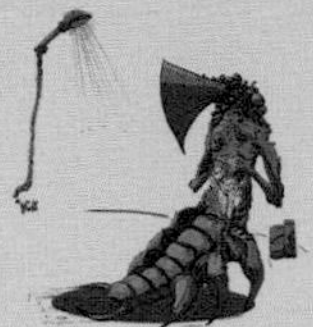

Boiler

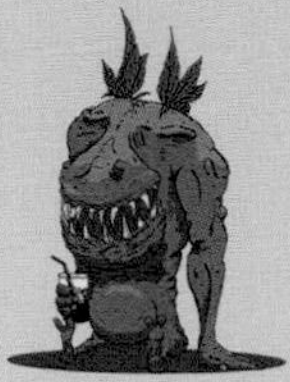

Cola

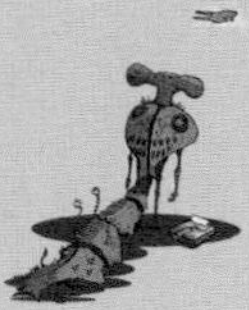

Damp

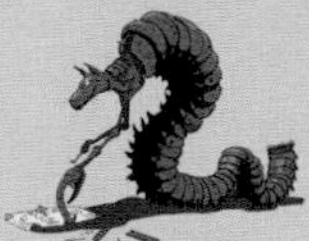

Extraneous

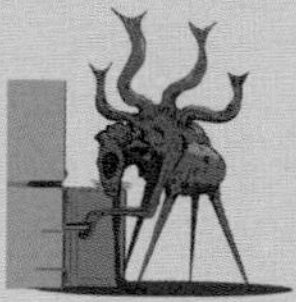

Freezer

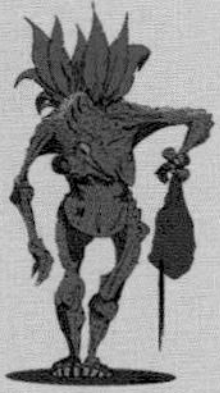

Garbage

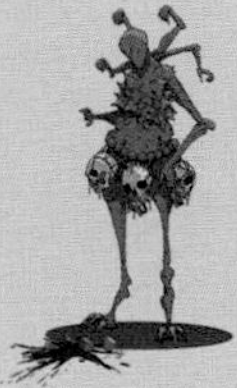

Handle

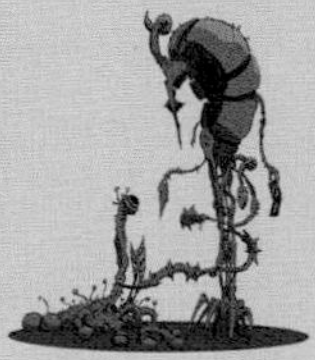

Immersive

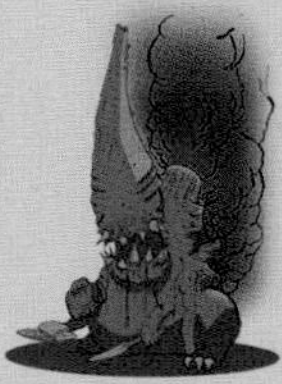

Jar

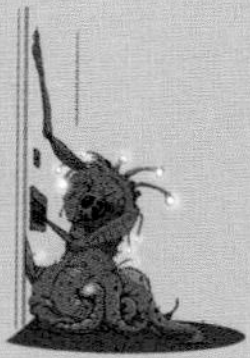

Keys

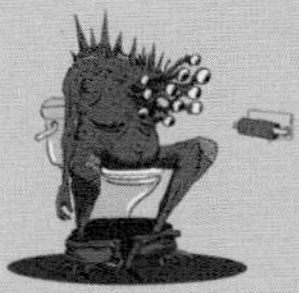

Lavatory

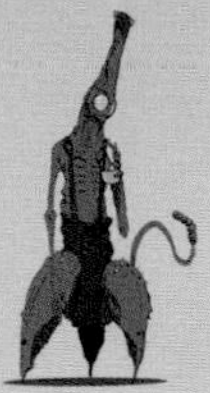
Milk

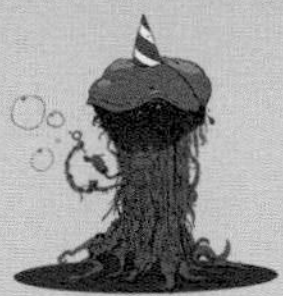
Nobody

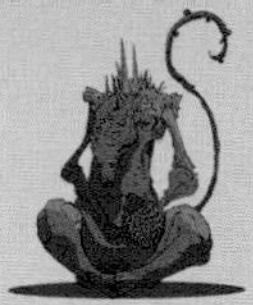
Overpriced

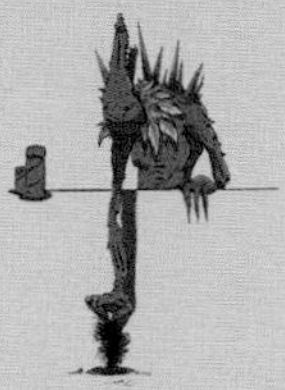
Plughole

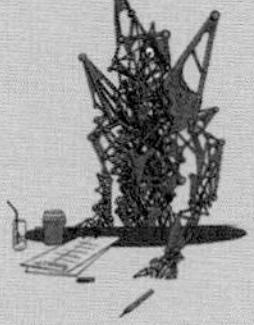
Quiz

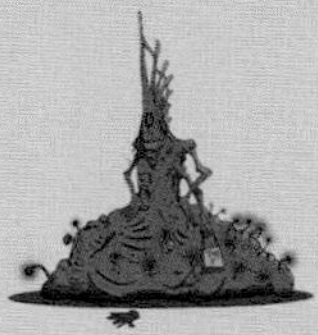
Receipt

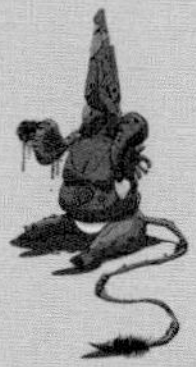
Sandwich

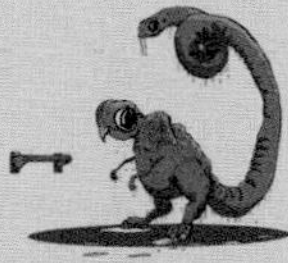
Towel

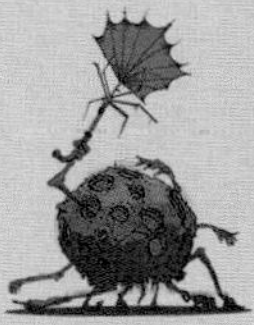
Umbrella

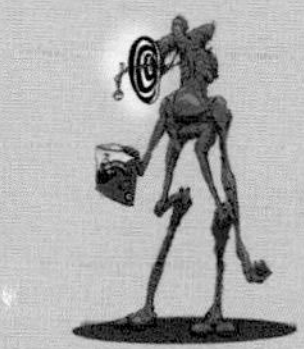
Vegetables

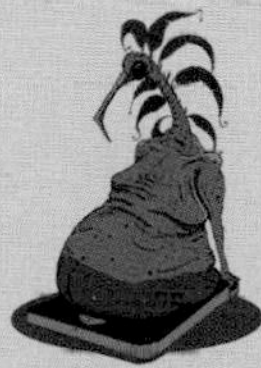
Weight

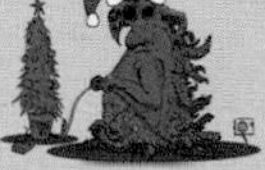
Xmas

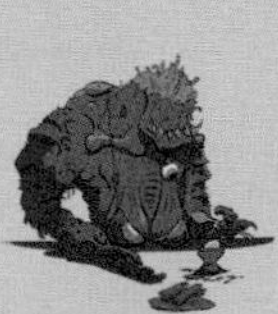
Yolk

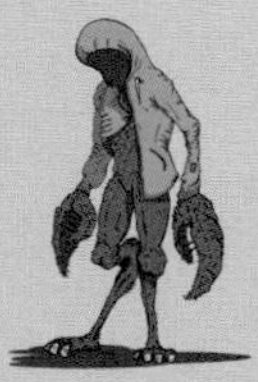
Zipper

Bonus

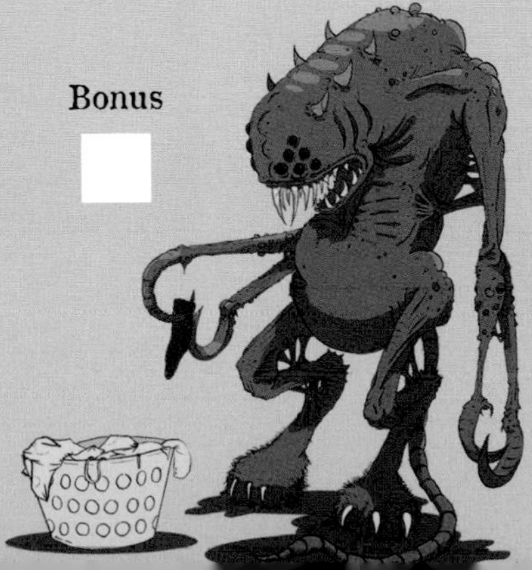

WHAT ARE YOUR DISAPPOINTED MONSTERS?

A ....

B ....

C ....

D ....

E ....

F ....

G ....

H ....

I ....

J ....

K ....

L ....

M ....

N
O
P
Q
R
S
T
U
V
W
X
Y
Z

AMMONITE
PRESS

www.ammonitepress.com